A Love Story:

EQ & JJJ

A Love Story:

FJV & PLB

Finding Love in Your 80s and 90s

To love is nothing.
To be loved is something.
But to love and be loved
is Everything.

By

Frank John Vernberg and Patricia Beckler

Ideas into Books ®
WESTVIEW
Kingston Springs, Tennessee

***Ideas into Books*®**
W E S T V I E W
P.O. Box 605
Kingston Springs, TN 37082
www.publishedbywestview.com

ISBN 978-1-62880-194-1

First edition, Valentine's Day 2020

Printed in the United States of America on acid free paper.

Contents

1. The Question

Grow old along with me!
The best is yet to be,
The last of life,
for which the first was made.
Our times are in his hand.

Robert Browning

Our first birthday celebration together:
Pat's birthday, June 14, 2016

2

FJV to PLB "I don't know! What do you want to do?" This profound question we frequently asked. We, Patricia Beckler and John Vernberg, are two residents in the Wildewood Downs Retirement Community, Columbia, SC. We met here and developed an interpersonal relationship in what is commonly called "Late in Life". We felt we were united by the mysterious machinations of fate which is the subject of this memoir, the story of beginning a new life in our eighty and ninety years of age!

PLB to FJV Yes, Sweet Love, those are the questions: *"What do we think?"* *"What do we want to do?"* Since you suggested that we write a book together, each composing alternate sections, I have been thinking how to go forward. Since this was YOUR idea, YOU must take the lead. I will follow (sort of)!

FJV to PLB Our answer to the question of "What do you want to do?" Well, let's write the Great American Biography of how two "elderly" individuals are exploring their life together in the advanced stage of their human life cycle. Of general note, many demographic studies have stressed there is an ever increasing number of elderly inhabitants in the world. What are they going to do?

Perhaps we can serve as a model of what can be done or should not be done! Maybe our struggles with worldly existence can contribute to the understanding of and adaptation to what life in the golden years might be like. Besides, it turned out to be more enjoyable than having extended conversations with others about nightly calls of nature or pictures of our grandchildren! In addition, we both have published books about our personal exploits and know something about the problems of authorship. Patricia, you have written about your life with your husband, John, during his end of life battle with dementia--Alzheimer's. My memoir, *IT'S A LONG STORY*, is about my first ninety years on Planet Earth.

Before delving into the present day description of our coping with everyday adventures, let's briefly outline our earlier lives so our present day actions can be understood.

John calls this "The Adoration Picture."

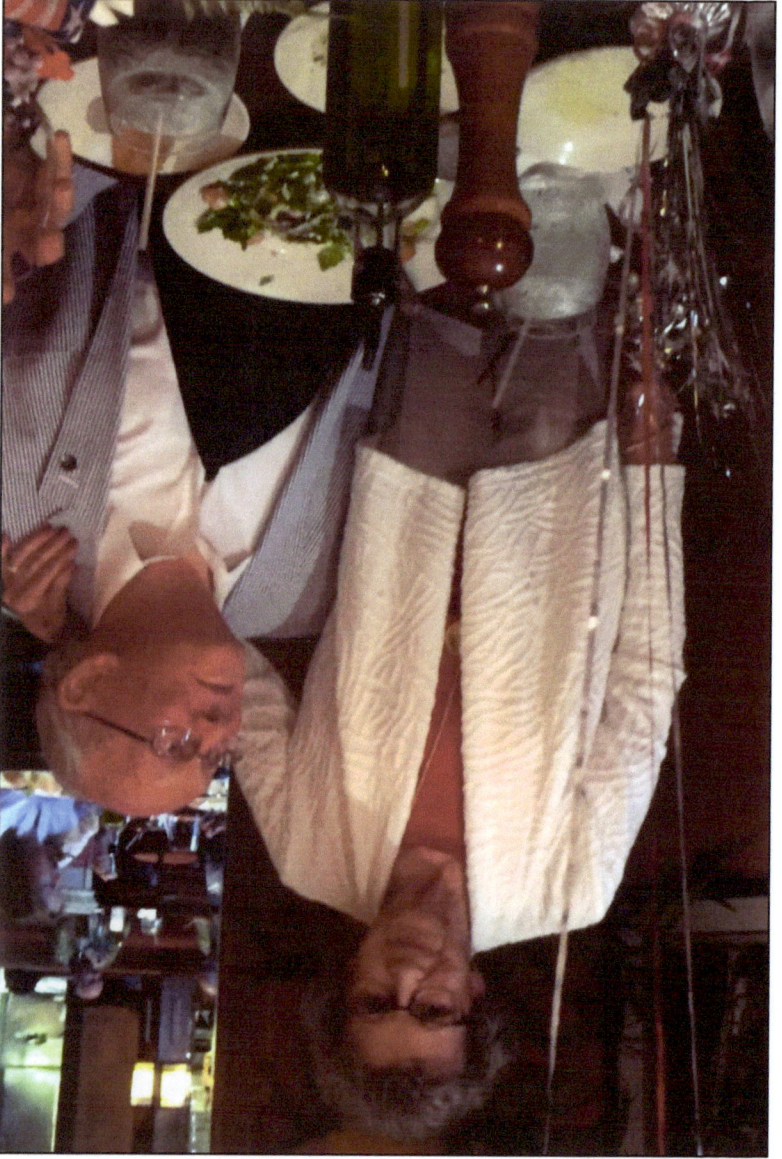

2. Early Life

Growing older
isn't so bad
if you do it
with someone
you love ...

A special dinner at Wildewood Downs.

FJV to PLB

November 6, 1925–1996

On a freezing, snow-covered day in November, 1925 (November 6 to be precise), I was born in Fenton, Michigan, a small town near the industrial city of Flint. My father was a tool and die maker; my mother, a housewife. Two years later my only sibling, a girl, Betty Lou, was born. Throughout her life we were extremely close sharing many high peaks of joy and low depths of despair. She died May 23, 2011. My father, Sigurd, was born in Stockholm, Sweden, February 17, 1899, and migrated to America February 15, 1918. Although my mother was born in New York City April 14, 1907, her parents were natives of Sweden.

Although my early days were during the depression, I don't remember being poor. Everyone was. Most of my early life was spent in Detroit, except for a year in the Bronx, New York, and several summers in the Catskill Mountains in New York living with my grandparents.

Emerging from the depression, my father had full employment and we had a middle class existence. My parents were Democrats. I graduated from Edwin Denby High School in June, 1942 and worked for a year in a dental laboratory being a gofer before enrolling in Wayne State University in September, 1943. I was drafted and served in the United States Navy from January, 1944 until June, 1946 as a hospital corpsman.

PLB to FJV

June 14, 1932--December 22, 1956

Since you have started with your early life, I will do the same.

Yes, of course, I was born! I entered this world in a small town, Dover, Tennessee, June 14, 1932. My parents were Mayme and Brandon Lewis. My brother, William Brandon, Jr. followed March 11, 1937. We had a nice house with a large lawn, adjacent to the Dover Elementary School. My grandmother, Mignonette Lewis, (Miss Minnie) lived on the other side of the school. The two years I was enrolled there, I would ask to run to her house briefly. My teachers understood that I preferred to use her bathroom rather than the "facilities" at the school.

The middle of a depression is not a good time to be born, or to raise a family for that matter! Struggling to establish a new law firm in the small town setting of Dover, Tennessee, through some connections, my Dad was able to secure the position, Clerk of the Federal Court, in Nashville, Tennessee. So, off we went. Thus, I became a "city girl". Not knowing what my life would have been, had we remained in Dover, I feel certain many opportunities opened to me that would not have occurred otherwise. Primarily, my long marriage to John Beckler and that whole rich and blessed life of fifty-four years.

I recall two things from my Dad's years in the Federal Court. First, Daddy was horrified one morning to hear the judge's secretary answer the phone,

"No, the judge is not in! Ha, he hasn't rolled over yet!" Short career for her! Later, in my short career teaching 8th and 9th graders, I took my classes to the US naturalization services held in "Daddy's court". During those years, 1955-56 specifically, many Europeans who had come to this country to escape the ravages of WW II were seeking US citizenship. Many had horrific stories of escaping the Nazi terrors. A real "learning experience" for my young natural-born Americans, hopefully demonstrating the great blessings of living in our democracy, now being sought by these immigrants, grateful for new lives in our wonderful country.

In Nashville, we lived on Baxter Avenue, across the street from Jere Baxter Elementary School. From there I went to Isaac Litton High School, graduating with a large class of several hundred. My favorite thing in high school was being co-editor of the student newspaper, THE LITTON BLAST, as I recall. I think my English teacher saw some potential in me that I hope I later fulfilled. Being a good Methodist, I went to Martin Methodist Junior College in Pulaski, Tennessee, before attending and graduating from Vanderbilt University in 1954, majoring in English and minoring in History.

Somehow, I obtained an editing job in New York City. I worked for the Woman's Division of the Methodist Church. Sometime later, *the women were invited to join the church,* so to speak, and the Woman's Division was incorporated into the overall administrative structure of the church. If I recall correctly, mission work at that time was within Woman's Division, so it was rather large. It had a large building in New York City so, living on 85th Street, I had my first experience of truly urban life. My job there was to edit, mostly shorten, a mission study book entitled FIVE SPIRITUAL CLASSICISTS. Never having even heard of one or two, I shudder to think of the abuse I inflicted on these early theologians! In my defense, I will say I later determined that it was a poorly written book to begin with. Incredibly, I was offered a permanent job there! It was tempting, but I listened to that inner voice, calling me back home to teach. A life-determining decision, to be sure.

My three-year teaching career went quickly. I taught at a new school, Madison Junior High, and felt fully initiated that first year when I realized that those experienced, supportive teachers had gotten all the good students and left me with the rest! My most interesting moment was when I took a switchblade knife from a passed-along eighteen-year old, a real misfit in this ninth grade English class. I enjoyed teaching, worked hard, and think I did a fairly decent job for a novice. I lived at home with my parents and had plenty of time for preparation.

3. Marriage and Family

> The aged do not walk naked into old age but clothed in the experiences of a lifetime!

Pat's first family event with the Vernbergs.

FJV to PLB

1945–1996

In September, 1945 I was married to one of my shipmates, Winona M. Bortz, a WAVE. After being discharged from the Navy, we enrolled in DePauw University, 1946 to 1949, and I was awarded a B.S. and M.S. in Zoology. Then we enrolled in Graduate School at Purdue University where we both were awarded a Ph.D. in Zoology in August, 1951.

Fortunately I joined the Duke University faculty in August, 1951, where I remained for eighteen years serving as Professor of Zoology. In August, 1969, I left Duke to become the Baruch Professor of Marine Biology and Director of the Baruch Institute of Marine Science, University of South Carolina. I retired from the faculty having served as interim Dean of Science and Mathematics, Dean of the School of the Environment, and Baruch Institute Director. My wife, who was the Dean of the School of Public Health and interim Provost, also retired. Both of us retired after twenty-seven years of service at USC. Coupled with our time at Duke University, we had been faculty members at an institution of higher education for a total of forty-five years.

During these forty-five years of servitude as a University faulty member, we had three children, Marcia, Eric, and Amy, They were with us during our many travels, including living a year in Jamaica and another year in Brazil where they attended various schools. Two of our offspring have PhD's (Eric in clinical psychology; Amy in International business. She also has a law degree.) Marcia has an Education Specialist Degree. They have married and we have six grandchildren and seven great grandchildren.

PLB to FJV

December 22, 1956--April 1984.

The most significant happening of that period of time was when mutual friends, thinking that Pat Lewis and John

Beckler belonged together, arranged a blind date. The rest, as they say, is history. John was in service by this time, fulfilling his ROTC obligation. We had courted initially in his old green car or in my Dad's car prior to his graduation from Vanderbilt, receiving a MS degree. John was stationed at Fort Gordon, Augusta, Georgia, when we married on December 22, 1956. Ever the problem-solver, JDB, knowing I would not have enjoyed the small, un-air-conditioned apartments on the base, found a charming pool-side cottage in town. Thus, we had privacy as well as comfort.

Since 2nd Lt. Beckler would be released from duty in late October, 1957, I went home in preparation for the birth of our first daughter, Cheryl Annette. My Mother was so nervous, I drove us to Nashville's Baptist Hospital for the big event, September 20, 1957. John arrived a few days later, staring in wonder at our first baby girl.

Those were the days when most deserving job-seekers received numerous offers, John applied to five large industrial companies, received offers from all five, and accepted the offer from Tennessee Eastman Company, a division of Eastman Kodak, in Kingsport, Tennessee. The companies I remember included Sherwin Williams Paint Company in Chicago and DuPont somewhere in Virginia. So, with a five-week old baby, we established our first home in Kingsport and remained a faithful Kodak family for many years. Completely separated from families for the first time, we quickly found a wonderful group of other young couples, mostly Eastman related, and had a solid, caring fellowship community. We were having babies, finding churches, buying permanent homes, basically living the good life and grateful for that. Our second daughter, Celia Arlene, was born March 21, 1959.

We were pushed to accomplish this, but we purchased 1522 Linville Street in the beautiful, older neighborhood of Fair Acres, in time for Cheryl to begin first grade within the Kingsport City School System, a priority for us at the time. The girls attended Lincoln Elementary, John Sevier Junior High and Dobyns-Bennett High School before going off to college. Cheryl received her nursing degree at East Tennessee State University in Johnson City. Celia graduated from Tennessee Tech in Cookeville, Tennessee with a degree in Accounting. Coincidentally, John had also completed his undergraduate work at Tennessee Tech.

Life during these years of raising our girls was good. They were involved in school activities, scouts, band, youth groups at church, various friends! <u>Boy friends</u>: I think there are advantages to having girls. We encouraged the girls to bring the boys home when feasible. We let them have the primary TV area on date nights (better than Lover's Lane). Even took a couple to the beach one year. My thought was...let the girls see these boys in OUR setting. Do they fit? Are they comfortable? Are WE comfortable? There were the horses, of course. I thought as long as the horses come before the boyfriends, that's a good thing at this age! Whatever our strategy was, it worked as they both married fine young men who made good husbands for our daughters.

During those important years I began my years of "Volunteerism" serving as PTA President, having various responsibilities in the American Association of University Women, Garden Club, numerous church activities. We never scrimped on baby sitters permitting us to have an enjoyable social life. Meanwhile, John's career began an upward climb. As witness to the kind of person he was, our friends always seemed happy with his advancement and continued to be our friends as the years went by.

Enjoying fine dining at Wildewood Downs.

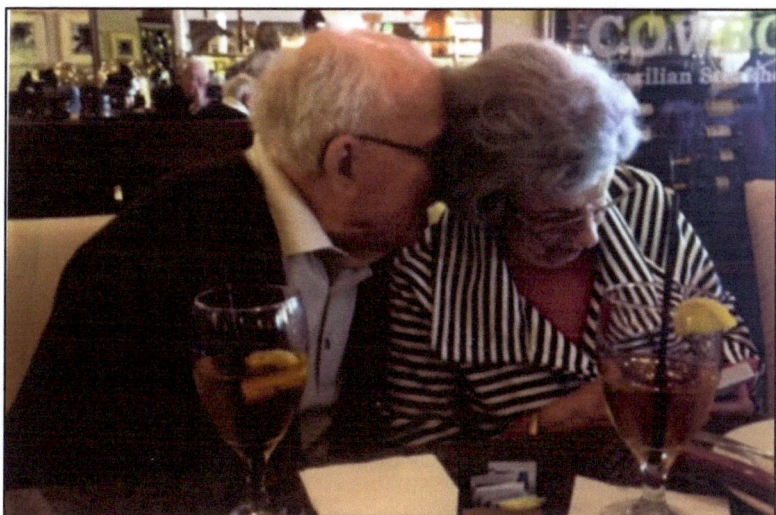

Check your email later.

4. On the Road Again

Happily ever after
works
one day at a time...

At the top of Mt. Pisgah.

PLB to FJV

April 1984--April 1, 1996.

I will never forget that Monday morning in April, 1984. I had my hand on the phone intending to call our travel agent and book my latest European trip. Not to be! The phone rang. John had just been made President of Carolina Eastman Company, and we were on our way to Columbia, South Carolina! Talk about mixed feelings!!! Celia, whose wedding was coming up, would continue to live in Kingsport with her Eastman-employed husband. Cheryl and Moi's children were coming along and visiting us often. The very next week I was house-hunting in Columbia! We moved July 10, 1984. One good thing...this move would place us midway between our daughters and their families. Columbia quickly became a convenient meeting place.

One dear, elderly friend said to me, somewhat tearfully, "Pat, do you think you will be happy in Columbia?" I said, "Frankly, Jackie, I don't see that I have a choice!" By that, I meant that I believed that God had already blessed us in so many ways, that now He wanted us in Columbia! Yes, emotionally, it was wrenching, but if you are doing what you think you are supposed to be doing, the strength you need is there.

Life in Columbia opened many doors! John was at his peak of energy career-wise. We had a beautiful home in one of Columbia's premiere neighborhoods. I was deeply involved in and enjoying many women's activities. We loved our church and quickly became part of the major leadership there. We were mid-way between our children. We traveled a lot, and I was able to do even more international travel on my own. The years went quickly until retirement began to approach.

FJV to PLB

LIFE IN SALUDA 2000–2008

Four years after retiring we sold our Columbia domicile and moved to our mountain home in Saluda, NC, which we purchased in 1989 as a vacation getaway from the campus madness. One of the items on our Retirement Bucket List was to travel extensively. Although our careers involved foreign travel, we determined to achieve two objectives of our future travels:

1) To visit the major ecosystems in the world to observe firsthand the outstanding diversity of the life forms and their habitats, including the Great Barrier Reef of Australia, the tropical rainforest of the Amazon, the freshwater wetlands of the Pantanal of Brazil, and the Serengeti Plains of Tanzania; and

2) To observe major cultural/ historic sites to help reestablish the balance between science and culture in our intellectual lives.

Our travels took us to the four corners of the Earth and from the Arctic to the Antarctic, to all the continents and to fifty-five countries. Various family members representing four generations traveled with us on many of our trips.

The yard outside Pat's front door.

5. Grief and Loss

If I should ever leave you
whom I love——
to go along the silent way,
grieve not,
nor speak of me with tears,
but laugh and talk of me
as if I were beside you there.
(I'd come - I'd come,
could I but find a way!
But would not tears and
grief be barriers?)
And when you hear a song
or see a bird I loved,
please do not let the
thought of me be sad
for I am loving you just as
I always have....

You were so good to me!
There are so many things
I wanted still to do
so many things
to say to you....
Remember that I
did not fear...It was
Just leaving you
that was so hard to face...
We cannot see beyond
but this I know
I loved you so
'twas heaven——
here with you!

Isla Richardson

Sunset at Wildewood Downs.

PLB to FJV

Retirement, Dementia, John's Death on September 13, 2010

With the benefit of lengthy recall and reflection, I realize that there were early signs of the approaching dementia, easily mistaken for the winding down of a long career. Needing frequent schedule reminders, missing appointments, even getting lost downtown, all alerting us to what would lead to our fourteen-year journey of forgetting. Dreadful, unrelenting, heart-breaking. My sweet husband died September 13, 2010, having been in a coma for five days, not recognizing any of us. I have told this story in my little book, *THE LONG GOODBYE*. To date, I have now given away around 1500 copies. Volunteer donations to the Alzheimer's Association from recipients now total over $23,000. Supporting the search for a cure has become a major commitment for me. We must find a cure in order to spare families and loved ones from experiencing what our sweet family *endured. Important research is happening at the University of South Carolina School of Medicine. I have great appreciation for their efforts, have even been out to visit the lab and have seen the little mice! And pray for them to be successful!*

FLY TO PLB

Without Winona

October, 2008–August 18, 2015

Shortly after returning to Saluda in mid-October, 2008, from an extended trip to the west coast of South America, Winona found a swollen lymph node in her left groin region. Upon examination, her physician recommended she meet with an oncology surgeon. The next morning we met with him. After a CAT Scan, an operation was scheduled. The infected lymph node was diagnosed as being lymphoma. The site of the lymph node was swollen and the hematoma was treated. At the Christmas holiday activities of our family who had assembled for our traditional family gathering, Winona did not display her usual unlimited energy. However, she was alert and interacted with everyone. There was no hint of her imminent death. Two days later she returned to the hospital and died the morning of December 29, 2008. On January 9, 2009, she would have been eighty-five years old. We had been married for sixty-three years and had had a rich, full life together. Naturally her sudden death was a devastating shock to everyone. Hundreds of well-wishers attended memorial services for her in Saluda and on the USC campus in Columbia, SC.

A period of mourning followed when family interaction gradually adapted to life without Winona. To indicate that family activities would continue, a gathering was held in Rockport, Massachusetts, during early August, 2009, when many martini toasts to Winona were downed.

Although trips involving the entire family ceased, travel by subsets of the family were undertaken. My desire to travel great distances did not disappear, but, my locomotor ability had diminished. In February, 2010, I took Amy on an exceptional Elderhostel trip to New Zealand. This wonderful country has a rich diversity of ecological ecosystems, ranging from snow to ice-covered areas in the south to semi-tropical northern habitats. This trip was followed by a Viking River Cruise of the Danube River in July, 2010, with Amy and children, Haley and Andrew.

Following the death of Winona, I gradually felt the need to move to a retirement community environment. After considering various options, I moved to Columbia, a place where we had lived with our family after we left Duke University in August, 1969. I had many friends there and felt that I was returning home; however, my strong ties to Saluda were not to be broken. I did not sell my Saluda home. With the help of Marcia, we listed the home with Vacation Rentals By Owner (VRBO), an international rental agency. The rental income helps pay the costs associated with maintaining a second home.

If, for some weird reason, more information is required about my life, it can be found in my published book, *IT'S A LONG STORY*, a memoir of my first 90 years of life. It is available from Amazon.

Birthday night celebration at Wildewood Downs.

.

6. A New Life

> The more I think about it,
> the more I realize there is
> nothing more artistic than
> to love others...

St. Patrick's Day, 2016.

FJV to PLB

August 18, 2015–February 9, 2016

The die is cast! Today, August 18, 2015, 7:15 am, is moving day. The moving van, Two Men and a Truck, is here and the two movers are busily loading my worldly possessions that will furnish my new bachelor quarters in WWD. It was a difficult task to select the furnishings to take and which to leave. Thanks to the advice of my female offspring, who love to manage everything, a detailed plan had been devised and became operational. The men finished loading the truck, left Saluda about 10:30 and arrived at Apartment 102C, WWD at 2:45. A welcoming committee, sans band, greeted them like they were delivering the cash prize from Publishers Clearing House.

Hectic unloading activities followed, including frank family discussions and harsh language about positioning of furniture and wall hangings. The next few days were devoted to unpacking and stocking the larder with household supplies. Then my family members left and I was alone in a foreign habitat. I undertook the responsibility of exploring this habitat to determine both its physical characteristic and its biological diversity.

Located in northeast Columbia in the middle of the WildeWood community, Wildewood Downs consists of thirty-seven acres of a former polo field. Within its confines, it has Patio and Garden homes, along with apartments for independent living. There are also Assistant Living facilities and Long Term Care areas. My apartment building consists of thirty apartments. My apartment includes two bedrooms (one serves as my study/office/guest room), dining and living area, kitchen, pantry, and laundry room. The area of the entire apartment is 1,175 sq. ft. The apartment entrance door opens to an indoor corridor that connects to the central club house where the main dining room, pub, card room, exercise room, library, sitting room, and offices are located.

The biotic diversity of WWD includes *Homo sapiens*, a few small dogs and house cats, waterfowl in the various ponds, an occasional fox (perhaps a survivor of earlier fox hunts), and migratory birds. The indigenous human residents range in age from 60-95 with a few centenarians. The sex ratio varies from 1.25 males to 8.5 females.

During any moment in time, you can review what happened to you previously, whether it is what I had for breakfast this morning or what happened at the high school prom forty-five years ago. Of course as you age more events occur resulting in experiencing layers of information and taxing your memory storage system. How many gigabytes do you have? For me, ninety-three years of living and surviving an unknown number of events (a number even greater than that of the USA national debt) create a gigantic data bank that influences how and what new data is processed. What response do I make to my new life in WWD?

I felt the need to assess my life and ask what do I want to do when I grow up? I have accumulated a mental closet of quotes dealing with almost every aspect of living. "Do unto others..." "Step on a crack you break your mother's back." "A penny saved is..." This is not a worthless football season. It is a building year." One dominant thought for me was how do you deal with loneliness.

What is loneliness? Is it a quantitative temporal quality? Is it experienced 100%, 25%, 10% of your time? Does it occur seasonally? Is it in competition with other feelings? The Oxford American Dictionary states: lonely, adjective, sad because one has no friends or company.

During my previous life, I had adapted to being socially lonely, although it was not a pathological response. I don't know when I first felt lonely and without friends. Perhaps because during my formative years we moved frequently. I was thrust into a new social environment and had to establish relationships with a new set of neighbors and school group of humans. I was shy and slow to interject myself forcefully into a leadership role. In retrospect, I feel that my pattern of developing friends was generally one of slow evolution from being a loner until I became better informed of the type of social dynamics of individuals in my new habitat. For example, in some groups one person will dominate the group's activities orally or physically. In general my approach was to develop an early friendship with the smartest and/or strongest kid in the group. This strategy was helpful in an unpleasant situation involving a bully. As a backup if this approach was not possible, I had developed my running skills which helped me to be on my high school track team (dashes and hurdles).

However, one of my lonely experiences occurred when I was drafted to serve in the US Navy in WWII when I was eighteen years old. A small number of us draftees from Michigan was sent to boot camp in Sampson, NY. I was assigned to a company of 120 individuals, many from upstate NY. Unfortunately, many of my new shipmates seem to dislike me and attempts to approach them were resisted. I was alone, friendless and had no idea of my future where and for how long would I serve in the military! Gradually I found out I was treated as an outcast chiefly because my brothers in arms thought Vernberg must be Jewish. Many upstate New Yorkers thought Jews were to be ignored. Over time I became an accepted member of the company. However I became deeply aware of what it felt like to be discriminated against.

The initial loneliness after the death of a loved one is a drastic period of existence. Although family and friends are a blessing, you wake up at 2:00 AM and you are alone. You miss physical and emotional involvement with your lost loved one. Although you face your newfound loneliness and make adjustments, you are still lonely and face a new future alone.

PLB to FJV

July 3, 2008--October, 2015

Moving to Wildewood Downs became an important decision when taking care of our large home and yard, along with the more complicated care required by John's illness, became more and more difficult. I knew that the various levels of care we would need were available at this facility, located just a short distance away. I was able to secure two lots and was able to build a larger home than the smaller patio homes. We moved, or rather I did with Cheryl's help. Celia had taken John to her home in Kingsport while the actual move took place.

Life at Wildewood Downs was much simpler with housekeeping, meal service and landscaping provided. In addition, I still had the benefit of our longtime housekeeper/caregiver, Marilyn Williams.

47

Thus, I was able to continue the various activities I still enjoyed and was also able to travel. Marilyn's husband, David, was always ready to help as well. John lived at home with me the first couple of years we were here. Eventually, I moved him to the Memory Care unit here. He was there about five months prior to his death in Long Term, September 13, 2010. Again, I refer to my book for the story of his death and our subsequent celebration of his life.

Living alone in my Wildewood Downs home was not so lonely given the shared communal life of a retirement facility. Dinner in the dining room each evening, the many activities, in addition to my off-campus involvements, kept me busy and as fulfilled as one can be when one's beloved spouse is no longer present. I continued to travel as well as enjoyed the frequent visits of our growing family. To my precious five grandchildren, their three husbands and six children, my "greats" were added!

7. Enchantment

we make
such
lovely memories
together

Life of Leisure!

FJV to PLB

Reflections

Once I had an overview of the spatial characteristics of my new habitat and even knew the location of such vital places as my apartment, the main dining hall, and the Pub, I began a socio-economic study of WWD. To assist in this unscientific endeavor, I took advantage of a great service provided by the administration. Each new arrival is assigned a mentor who not only explains the idiosyncrasies of the community but introduces you to many of the indigenous inhabitants and arranges dinners with them. Also I learned of the many existing programs which foster a spirit of friendliness and social interaction. These include bridge, yoga, exercise classes, bingo, book club, putting on the green, field trips to local sites of interest, and happy hour in the Pub, just to name a few examples.

The residents represent a diverse background including business executives, academics, physicians, mothers, military personnel ranging from a general or two to officers and enlisted members. Females outnumber males. The number of married couples, widows, and widowers varies.

Fortunately I was able to meet and befriend many of my newfound neighbors within a reasonably short period of time. Having lived in Columbia for thirty-one years before moving to Saluda, NC, I found a good basis for mutual topics for discussion.

Almost as if being guided by fate, I was strongly attracted to one individual, Mrs. Patricia Beckler, a widow who had lived in WWD for several years and knew most of the residents. Our paths crossed with increasing frequency, and she invited me to one of her gala dinners held in her home. When she and her husband John moved to WWD from their home in neighboring development of WildeWood, they were able to build a 3,000 sq. ft. home. This is the largest home in WWD. He died September 13, 2010 of Alzheimer's complications.

Leading up to our February 9, 2016, informal Proclamation of Interdependence, we had numerous informal talks about our separate but equal interests, likes, and dislikes. We found we could and did have conversations in which we could frankly agree or disagree at a level of openness and honesty. We shared experiences each of us had during our marriages. Pat had been married fifty-four years and I, sixty-three years.

Soon we began seeing each other regularly, especially for dinner. Finally we decided on February 9, 2016, that we were seriously enchanted with each other. I suggested that she finally wore me down and caught me.

PLB to FJV

WHO CAUGHT WHOM???

February 9, 2016--Present

"I wore YOU down and caught YOU." Surely your sense of honesty compels you to revise the accuracy of that statement!

Once the holidays were over, we were both included in a festive birthday celebration in Springdale Hall in Camden. That's when it happened for me. I think it had already happened for you, John, beginning at my Christmas Dinner. One afternoon in early February, you invited me to your apartment for tea. I still remember that sweet moment as I was leaving. A serious conversation followed a few days later in which I needed to know your wishes and intentions. Although it was a little "wordy", you were clear in expressing your wish that we spend more time together, including dinner each evening. You were quick in making that happen.

8. Interdependence

What I give to you
 and you give to me
cannot be boxed and
 put under the tree
but we both know it's there,
 as does Heaven above
It's that wonderful intangible
 we know as Love

EWS

That wonderful intangible we know as love.

FIV

Reflections

The development of our strong relationship occurred over several mutual areas of interest, over a period of time. It was a gradual process of being together pursuing different activities and then suddenly realizing that we were a couple, we were friends, we were magnetically and physically attracted to each other. We were in love.

To reinforce our desire to strengthen our personal inter-dependence and our need for community involvement, we participated in a number of events, including: South Carolina Philharmonic, the USC Symphony, Broadway in Columbia (i.e. *Chicago*, *Wizard of Oz*, *Book of Mormon*), Palmetto Opera and Columbia Baroque. In addition WWD sponsored tours for residents of local historic and cultural sites, such as Camden Battlefields, South Carolina Statehouse and the University of South Carolina campus.

I do not know the moment that I knew I loved her. No great clap of lighting was reported by CNN or the Dow Jones did not record a new high or low. I do remember that I (the spider) invited Pat (the fly) to my apartment for a cup of tea (caffeine-free). As she rose to leave, I had an uncontrollable urge to kiss her. Naturally I did the gentlemanly thing and I kissed her!! A few days later our Proclamation of Interdependence was agreed to.

PLB to FJV

I do not know the exact moment we knew we loved each other. I think you knew first. How could I resist your goodness, the tenderness with which you treat me? Yes, your humor, your intelligence and quick wit, your thoughtful ideas about ways we can be together, things we can do together! It seemed so natural to us. Obviously, it was an issue of some interest to our curious neighbors!

9. Connections

Love is not affectionate feeling, but a steady wish for the loved person's ultimate good as it can be obtained.

C.S. Lewis

Lunch at Top of Carolina, U of SC campus. The tall building in the background, The Heritage, is where John and Winona Vernberg lived for a few years following their retirement from the University of South Carolina. John had been Dean of Environment and Winona was Dean of Public Health. They were a power couple!

FIV

Reflections

During the process of developing a long-term relationship with Patricia, each of us encountered many obvious issues and a few unintended ones. The issue of companionship was just discussed, but many other issues arose which were important. I can't remember the sequence and hesitate to rank them in order of importance. However, these issues are somewhat interdependent and may influence each other. They are all a part of us and help distinguish our individual beings and the characteristics of our partnership. One individual plus one individual equals a new entity of our being an individual couple.

One issue that emerged early is what will our respective offspring think of their aging parents falling in love. Have they entered their second childhood and are in a puppy love phase? Should our children check our diets to see if we are taking some miracle herbs or fruit found in the Garden of Eden (perhaps apples!).

Pat and I individually broke the news using wiles learned over many years of dealing with our offspring (sometimes even successfully!). Their responses varied from 1) We knew already. What took so long? to 2) Are you sure? In my case, my three children were supportive and wanted details. They knew Pat and wanted to get better acquainted. With time, family interaction occurred—birthday parties, holidays, etc.

The question of marriage was confronted by us and after pros and con discussions we agreed that we would remain an unwed couple. We felt our love was complete and sufficiently strong enough to serve as marriage vows. Potential legal problems associated with mixing our separate families could be avoided without hampering the development of relationship between our two families.

PLB to FJV

Ah-h-h! Telling our children! I can name...and also love... the twelve adults that comprise "my immediate family." Yet, they have very busy lives. Also some enjoy long emails and frequent telephone calls more than others. Several are employed and have families of their own. So it was natural that I actually discussed this surprising development in my personal life with one of my daughters. Looking back, I think this was very important for several reasons.

First, this exchange presented me with an opportunity to analyze, in realistic terms, this surprising relationship in which I found myself and which had a growing meaning in my life. John Vernberg and I were not just friends, although we truly were serious friends! We were not just two people who enjoyed each other and having someone to do things with, although that was certainly true! We truly love each other. We cherish each other. We value each other. We feel surprisingly close to each other. I think, possibly because of our age and also our long experience as partners in a committed relationship, we sort of skipped some of the early get-acquainted stages in a growing relationship.

Second, it was important that I made it absolutely clear that I was not forgetting anyone! I was not replacing anyone! John Beckler had been a part of my life, a part of ME for over fifty years! Nothing would ever change that! I know how blessed my life has been, especially my married life. I believe, along with possible statistical support, that for those of us who have had long, strong marriages, we know what we have lost. It cannot be REPLACED. Yet, for the one left alone, life is not over. We have to find our way in a new life. Somewhere along the way, a dear friend wrote me a note saying how happy John Beckler would be to know my life had not ended with his death. That happiness, not just adjustment and contentment, could be

mine again. I believe that is true.
Bittersweet, yes! However, I believe the
nature and character of my beloved
husband was such, he would want my
happiness even if it meant, having lost
him, I could love again.

Thirdly, it is of supreme importance
to me that my loved ones, these twelve
adults, understand all this and accept
the realities of the moment. They love me
and, without exception, want the best for
me. They are also mature enough, and
polite enough, to be objective in their
observations. I hoped that, as they got
to know this older gentleman with this
strange name, they would find a place
for him in our shared lives. I believe they
have.

Monthly luncheon at Wildewood Downs.

10. Ramifications

The smiles turn to laughs, and laughs turn to kisses and before you know it, the days turn to weeks, and weeks turn into months and you'll find yourself forgetting what it was like before he was in your life...

Enjoying lunch off campus.

FIV

Reflections

February 9, 2016–Present

Establishing a loving relationship between Patricia and me involved a number of issues other then our primary love of each other. Many of these issues need attention between two individuals irrespective of age; but for elderly individuals, like us, they may be more acute because the elderly as a group are closer to the upper limit of their life cycle.

One such issue is finances. Each of us has a retirement plan that permits us to have a comfortable life style and to have wills to deal with the distribution of our estates after our death. We early decided that each of us would make financial arrangements independent of the other. One advantage of not marrying is that potential inheritance disputes can be avoided. Although other newly formed couples of the elderly may have more complex interactions, the issue of financial planning is important to avoid interpersonal problems.

Another issue facing "newly formed couples of the elderly" is living accommodations. If you start from the basic premise that each person currently has living quarters, then the question is "your place or mine" or do we keep our current separate living abodes? In our situation, we each have separate quarters in a retirement community. Patricia has a four bedroom house and I have a two bedroom apartment. These units are about 423.2 yards apart! We decided that initially we would keep our present separate accommodations subject to periodical review. My mountain home in Saluda, NC would continue to be jointly occupied.

Although we were sensitive about what our neighbors might say about our budding romance, we did not hide our being together much of the time. However, Patricia did not want me to park my car in her drive-way after 11:00. Frequently after dinner I would drive to her house until around 9:30 pm when I returned to my apartment.

Obviously, she thought the eyebrows of the very observant neighbors would be raised and their tongues wagging. As a prank I put a sign on her garage door— NO PARKING AFTER 10:00 pm. I think it caused more gossip. In time our friends realized we were a couple and accepted us as a couple.

Residents living in individual houses separated from the Clubhouse are provided with golf carts, permitting easy transport around the campus.

Many evenings we would get in Pat's cart and drive around the various streets checking for extremists, wild bears, and checking to see if the various water fountains in the large ponds were functioning properly. She would let me off at the west door of Apartment Building C. If the moon was in proper alignment with other celestial entities, I might get lucky and get a kiss or two. This door is now known as the Kissing Door.

PLB

Reflections

Developing a serious relationship at this age is quite an interesting experience. As I have said elsewhere, I have not been committed to anyone but John Beckler since I was twenty-four years old! This was new territory for me! Yet it seemed so natural and so good! How did it happen? Was it a gift? I don't believe in "fate" as an explanation of life's events. Yet there are many that don't have rational, objective explanations. I do believe that, for people of faith, there is the wish to live each day within the framework of our beliefs and being attentive to the presence and guidance of God, as He tenderly and lovingly watches over us. Thus, I am compelled to say that, for me, my relationship with John Vernberg is something that *God intended for us*. I believe that God, loving each one of us equally, prepared John to meet and love me, and that He prepared me to meet and love John Vernberg. It isn't necessary for anyone else to believe this. I believe it! It is right for me and is the reason that not a day goes by that I don't say a "thank-you" prayer for this sweet time in my life. With the husband I had, I think my standards are rather high. Yet, I recognize in John Vernberg goodness, intelligence, humor, thoughtfulness and many other characteristics that draw me to him. *Yes, it is a gift!*

Pat's first trip to Saluda.

11. Travel

Love is a tickling
sensation around
the heart!

Pat and John in Spain.

FIV

Reflections

Although we had independently traveled extensively overseas, we traveled together only once. In September, 2017, we and Marcia, John's daughter, journeyed to Spain (Madrid, Jerez, Conil de la Frontera) to visit with Amy (John's other daughter) who was on her honeymoon with her husband, Greg Harris. Later Pat and John and family members were booked on a 2018 Silver Seas cruise from Barcelona to Rome. Unfortunately, Pat was hospitalized and was unable to go with us. However, Pat and I have had numerous trips together in the southeastern United States. These trips allowed us additional opportunities to bond. Some of these trips were to our mountain retreat in North Carolina and to Tennessee and Georgia.

An important aspect of our relationship is that various activities allow us to independently pursue some activities. We continue to be individuals in addition to being a couple. Pat has lived in Columbia since1984 and is very active in numerous organizations including Shandon United Methodist Church, as a board member of Columbia Baroque, a member of the WildeWood Book Club, Shandon Book Club and The Aloise Society/Alzheimer Association. I am a member of University Associates and bridge clubs.

Lurking on the fringe of our daily life style agenda is the question of our health. At almost any phase of our life cycle our health is of paramount interest. However, as one ages, awareness of debilitating health issues and ultimately death is heightened. We have experienced the loss of a loved spouse and have firsthand experience of the life adjustment process. Not having a crystal ball in our possession, we don't dwell on the subject. We have reasonably good health and have good health care to deal with emerging problems. In addition, we have dealt with death procedures such as wills.

Among the many facets of an ever-increasing number of older inhabitants on earth, one area of concern is what do old people do with their lives when they enter their eighties and beyond. Are the present-day octogenarians the seventy-year-old individuals of yesterday and the nonagenarians former octogenarians? Modern medical developments appear not only to have extended the life span but also to have improved the health of the world population.

The tourism industry has catered to the demands of the elderly for improved facilities to enable them to travel. In addition, national and international legislation has been helpful to the handicapped, i.e., the 1968 Vocational Rehabilitation Act. Both of us have experienced these welcomed changes. Pat's last major junket was to the northwestern Pacific states of Oregon and Washington and the southwestern region of Canada. This trip took place when she was eighty-six years old. My last international cruise was from

Barcelona to Rome when I was ninety-three. Although these trips were successful and free of medical complications and general travel problems such as delayed/cancelled flights or weather delays, we have decided that our future lust to travel will be restricted to the many marvelous sites closer to our home base. This decision was predicated on several reasons. One – We have visited many of the regions of the world and interplanetary travel is not readily available. Two – Areas of the world we would like to visit are not safe for visitors, such as the early center of the world's history (i.e. Iran and Iraq). Three – Our bodies are less resistant to the rigors of travel. Oh, my aching back or where are the restrooms? Because the desire to see new habitats is deeply imbedded in our DNA, we will continue to keep expanding the borders of the bubbles we live in, even if we do so vicariously.

12. Rings

Love is friendship
that caught fire!

A summer day on the town.

PLB

Rings

Yes, we have exchanged rings! Not traditional wedding rings and not in the traditional way! One morning John drove me to Sandhills to do an errand. He stayed in the car while I went inside our local jewelers for some watch replacement batteries. As I waited, of course, I looked around at all the attractive displays. At some point I realized I was looking at men's rings! Not simple gold bands but beautifully created bands, silver and platinum, most designs very subtle and quite lovely. I told the jeweler I would be right back! "John, would you like a ring?" Without much comment, he joined me inside. As we chose one, he seemed quite pleased, putting our selection on his left hand. Hum, I said to myself. That should keep the other women away!

Yes, I now wear a beautiful ring which I received on my next birthday. Since I will always wear my wedding ring, given to me in 1956, I wear the ring from John Vernberg on my third finger, left hand, inside my wedding ring. It's an "outward and visible sign" that it's all right for me to have this new relationship in my life.

13. Life Goes On

> Being someone's first love
> is great, but to be their
> last is beyond perfect.

Thanksgiving Day, 2016,
Red Rocker Inn, Black Mountain, N.C.

PBL

Conclusion

So...what lies ahead? Of course, we do not know. But...we have never known. Yet life has been abundantly good to us both. Again, as a person of faith, I look back at my life and know God has always been there close—always available—even when I was inattentive to His loving presence. Why should the days ahead be different? I try to live each day grateful for this surprise blessing of my relationship with John Vernberg. This tender, sweet time that we call "A Love Story".

Thank You, God!

Thank you, my dear Dr. Vernberg!

I love you so very much!

FJV

Conclusion

"I don't know! What do you want to do?" This question began Chapter 1 and has challenged us to put on paper how two aging, but young at heart, individuals met and established a lifetime relationship. Our story is of the initial magnetic attraction and continuing convergent evolution of a young (octogenarian) woman and a maturing (nonagenarian) male.

Life Goes On!

We hope you have enjoyed our story!

Calligraphy

by

Polly Judd